Volume 63 of the
Yale Series of Younger Poets
edited by Dudley Fitts
and published with aid from
the Mary Cady Tew Memorial Fund

COMING CLOSE
AND OTHER POEMS

by HELEN CHASIN

Foreword by Dudley Fitts

Yale University Press
New Haven and London 1968

Acknowledgment is made to the following
publications for poems which originally appeared
in them:

The Atlantic Monthly: "In the Sea; In the Stream,"
"Deja Vu," "Seeing You Off"

Boston Magazine: "The Hippies of Harvard
Square," "Speculation on the Boston Strangler"
("Victim")

Poetry: "The Witch House at Salem: Winter,"
"Leaving, or Being Left," "An Empty Bed at
the Asylum"

To my parents

FOREWORD

'A brief Introduction explaining Why this particular manu-
script was chosen': the editorial directive is simple enough, but
the implementation of it is far from simple. Not that the pre-
liminary decisions are difficult to make: of the two hundred or
more manuscripts submitted annually, a dozen at most will
survive a cursory first inspection. The agony begins when your
dozen is reduced to the two or three—rarely more—that
emerge as the final contenders. What is the basis for judgment?
One's own taste, ultimately; which is another way of saying
'prejudice'. Both X and Y have something of significance to
say, and they have the technical competence to say it with
freshness and point. They are not portentous or idly eccentric,
they are not heartless. They can distinguish, moreover, be-
tween poetry and self-abuse: an increasingly rare accomplish-
ment. Both of them, it is true, have their special forms of
dottiness, their flaws, their clinkers. Who of the best of poets
does not? And X and Y are at the beginning of a career. One
of them must lose, according to the terms of this particular
competition, and 'I like X better than Y', the editor decides;
and acts. He is then asked to explain Why.

This Why, so far as my own procedure is concerned, has
usually found its justification in a general feeling about a group
of poems in a manuscript rather than in the collection as a
whole. In *Coming Close* (and it is time that this Introduction
took the hint) it was the delicate warmth, the amused inno-
cence, of Miss Chasin's love poetry that finally gave me my
decision.

> They claim they can
> smell evil and understand words. What
> illegal luck—

The perplexities of evil, the pain, move beneath the surface of
the best of these poems; the excitement comes from Miss

Chasin's ability to 'understand words' and set them dancing in a kind of ritual exorcism. 'Love's Game: *Go'*, for example:

> The stones
> of separate colors
> defeat me.
> I have no such thoughts.
>
> Telling the stones
> like rosaries:
> you, you, you.
>
> I am bound to lose
> this game.
> I do not choose
> to avoid
> enclosure.
>
> You may increase the space
> tenfold;
> never enough.
>
> The first move: complete
> statement. Others
> merely repeat.

The resonances are as grave as the laconic verse is guileless and composed—only apparently guileless, and 'composed' in all senses. My early reading of the manuscript kept coming back to this poem, finding in it a concentration of Miss Chasin's most persuasive qualities: warmth, as I have said; clarity; a true and delicate run of the line; and, most characteristically, a serious playfulness that dares much and that seems to me to succeed wholly. The poem is no apocalypse, it does not shake you; but its touch is sure and deep, and the touch, I find, remains.

There was, or there is, only one Phœnix, though Miss Chasin seems to acknowledge several:

> Mythic birds
> taste their own ashes, are something
> of their sometime selves after all.

and it is a *sigillum* of her work that it does taste its own emotional pain and rise restored. And refreshed, one adds: finding refreshment for oneself in these gentle transmutations of experience. The adjective may be offensive in an era of confessional plain dealing and screech, but I am talking about the civility of the central poems in *Coming Close*. There is no question of a muted mode. If you want to be knocked down, Miss Chasin can knock you down ('Addiction') and pick you up ('After Termination') and dust you off ('Joy Sonnet in a Random Universe') with an admirably deft wit. 'People are catching', she remarks. Who was the surrealist poet who pronounced that ELEPHANTS ARE CONTAGIOUS? People, at any rate, are catching, and in her pages she has caught herself, first of all, and investigated the catch with subtlety and a saving sense of comedy. The range is perhaps too much restricted, though she has nothing in common with the fashionable egolatrists who mistake their symptoms for the Gnawing of the Worm. It might be more accurate, however, to suggest that the in-closings of her poetry are in their effect impulses away from the centre of Self:

> In those days, days promised themselves
> like buds: pussy willows, yellow roses,
> lily of the valley, closed
> around their own joy, but
> everything possible, the air
> sweetened with clues. I could believe
> they might burst into the world
> like music, shattering stem, blossom,

clusters of bells—all previous light
small by comparison, space a paltry idea.
That could have happened, but
did not; now days
grow into themselves, tighten, and
shut: right, true as anything.

The motion seems to exclude, to move towards a central safety.
Paradoxically, however, the effect is one of extending radiation.
'In those days' is liturgico-elegiac; 'now days / grow into them-
selves' is elegiac without benefit of the liturgy'; but the poem
as a whole represents a conversion of impulse, a celebration of
joy in the very accents of regret. It was this kind of excitement,
'right, true as anything', that brought me to my decision about
Miss Chasin's book.

DUDLEY FITTS

CONTENTS

COMING CLOSE
AND OTHER POEMS

FIRST SIGHT

The first familiar easy face-to-face
says yes, this is what it is
and was, every hour of the thousand thousand
coming to this, because of us: a certain
unsurprising comfort, suddenly realized.
We are informed with one another like memory.

SUMMER MORNINGS

In those days, days promised themselves
like buds: pussy willows, yellow roses,
lily of the valley, closed
around their own joy, but
everything possible, the air
sweetened with clues. I could believe
they might burst into the world
like music, shattering stem, blossom,
clusters of bells—all previous light
small in comparison, space a paltry idea.
That could have happened, but
did not; now days
grow into themselves, tighten, and
shut: right, true as anything.

TELEMANN

(To A.C.)

Measure is a guess the mind makes about itself:
gestures and glimpses worked into confidence.

My daughter is excessive in her small age,
takes in the world like breakfast,
pricks the raw yolks of mornings
till they run like blood in her mouth.
Skin's a cage, or a fiction.
Names prowl in the tall grass, beasts
tamed into syllables:
cat's-paw, foxglove, hart's tongue.
Birds have gone south three times and come back.
She serves up fistfulls of powdered rock
to the sea, equitably pours hope
at the sand's perpetual teatime.

In music things begin and end,
spread, strain, and return into themselves,
are contained: behave well,
like lessons we have learned and been praised for.
Untutored in these comforts, my girl
has her small ways.

EARLY THAW

This season sets in like a condition.
I am succulent as agar to its green spread,
eagerly suck up its moist progress like mud;
everywhere liquids run sweet enough
to make the teeth ache, or kill sprouts
obedient in their pots.
How the tepid wind spills into the air
like nourishment, like messages;
and how it will remit, the warm
wet rampage over, and how
the cells will diminish
into safety.

ALONG THE WAY

Tombstones, photographs: the family convened
for an occasion, composed and facing out
against the lens
and now against my backward glance
for a glossy, cardboard moment. One Thanksgiving
they were stopped dead
and then resumed the quick and trivial grind
of plain days, leaving behind this marker,
this prediction.
             I am in the procession,
caught successively with scarred knees, orthodontia,
and cantaloupe belly, marks of progress, each
black-and-white minute, each assembly
a station in the dead march.

MOTION PICTURE

(To my Cousin)

In this instant we are less than life size,
a grainy frame in a home movie
thrown on a makeshift screen, recurring sequence
shrunk to a nervous still: in shoddy focus
you tease, I tag along.
Our jittery flick skips back to itself.
I tease. Your threat's
to ignite your Junior Chem-Lab set
and take me with you.
Won't love's holocaust suffice,
or must you commit trifles—
ambushes, skirmishes, grotesque tales
only a girl would suffer?

Our old film
flaps on its wheel. Fade
out. The end. I pick at motives
and dreams of broken men
like band-aids.

THE WORD *PLUM*

The word *plum* is delicious

pout and push, luxury of
self-love, and savoring murmur

full in the mouth and falling
like fruit

taut skin
pierced, bitten, provoked into
juice, and tart flesh

question
and reply, lip and tongue
of pleasure.

AMONG THE SUPERMARKET

Dearest, this abundance of tinned goods,
quick-frozen gourmet snacks, V-8 juice, plasti-
paks, imported tidbits in foreign grease,
megatons of detergent power
and jars of cloudy premixed cocktails
undoes me: instantly
I am kin to the national idiot
agency men count on: transfixed by canned music,
astonished in the aisles, dumbly convinced of
happiness, crazy to make meals
like making love.

My dear, it is not merely persuasion; not
coming to terms with all varieties,
each with its own use; not, stunned by choice,
compulsion to cram the cart, consuming until
even Brand X is familiar

but that I can still say, amid this ridiculous
array of food and ancillaries, displayed with super-
lunatic logic
the bounty of days and households is manifest.
Surrounded by these necessities, these
trivia, I find: love is possible. We could live
among its items. These found objects are its signs.

CAMBRIDGE AS METAPHOR

(to J.F.N.)

Often enough the town's sky hangs about
like a sullen child, giving offense.
You said
the sky's like paraffin:
dense, greasy, opaque,
saved out of previous seasons—
ugly but useful.
You poets are adept at making do
and more, as if it's easy
to blot up the moist and waxy air
because that serves your purpose.

IN THE SEA

*A woman pleasing to men is good only for frightening
fish when she falls into the water.*

Zen Proverb

Silver, glittery as scales, the sea shatters
and scratches; plummeting through my reflection
I scatter fish from the surface.
Down here their mouthing
measures my descent like a pulse.
Gills scull and feather; the cellulose eyes
are stupid and dull as death.

                        Greenish queen
of the sea, in ferny crown and watercress garment,
I turn, turn in the weeds, in the deep
spasm of tides, under the dark weight
where dumb, sightless, transparent forms
mumble and push, unamazed.

IN THE STREAM

Two monks, a Hindu and a Zen, came to a stream. The Hindu started to walk on the water. The Zen cried out: Come back! Come back! That is not the way to cross a stream.

Zen Story

Saffron-wrapped, swathed in white gauze, we two
pursue the pine-needle path of no path. We are here.
We may never arrive. Perhaps we have passed.
The stream glitters like amber, like jade,
like pieces of water. Persimmon fish
tremble and rush, nervous and easy as God.

Friend, it can be done: advancing on crystals
lo! we are over—our robes dry, spectacular.
But knowing water, choose the liquid way;
seeking God, wade into the water.
Our skirts bell out, go heavy and coarse,
the cold brushes our skin
with characters. Wet, literal
we are crossing.

THE WITCH HOUSE AT SALEM: WINTER

The cold burns like faggots.
Bodies burn at us,
hellish in their musky linen.
Rigid caps and dirty muslins move in the bare landscape,
visible as nests.
This is a bad place for secrets.
Starchy ministers march in their stiff course
toward God.
Human smells and promises twist in our nostrils;
men reek of their wants.
This house has witnessed rare performances.
At night pimply apprentices sweat in our lofts,
clotting straw with proofs of the devil's purpose.
Smiles wicked as wet dreams steam in our kitchens.
Evidence abounds. Babies sicken,
rocks cripple our blades. Virtuous girls—
Prudence, Mercy, Hope—close into scolds.
It proves unwise to prosper.
Evil roosts here and will not give over.
A grim bird cries
admit! admit!
There is no asylum.

DÉJÀ VU

God knows. That passion meant
plenty, at the time: timeless words whose intent
baffles me now. How I burned!
How did I come through? No matter. I learned
nothing, except: pain teaches nothing. Mythic birds
taste their own ashes, are something
of their sometime selves after all. All
is not lost even by our forgetting; words
testify in spite of us. Total recall
is not required. Once I said *always;* once
is enough, God knows, to establish relevance.

HORIZONTAL

Doctor X has wax in his third ear.   strophe
I've told him everything
he knows; he knows they'll all be
histories
mysteries
symbols
and sorry.

Doctor X has sex on the brain.   antistrophe
That's no place! I can say anything
he says, he says.
Associate
with him?
Feel free.
Don't worry.

ADDICTION

Daddy, the concern
in your expressed hope
that I'm not on the stuff's
extremely touching.
Would it be too much to guess
your guess:
who turned me on? what junkie
pressed his packet, fixed me
in his need until I moan
for his sweet sake? You liar,
love's a racket, at best
only a connection.
In your funky dreams
are pricks
like love-bites
the scars of my desire?

FALLING OUT

–tight, –proof, unavailable
in our capsule and turned off
to communiqués, we orbited
until our unit came apart, until

the old pull re-exerts.
I spill,
susceptible, in the human air.
Moving among bodies, bombarded with messages
already I commit it all, more
than could happen, turning historical
with strangers, living with passers-
by. Outside the gemini kingdom
people are catching.

THE RECOVERY ROOM: LYING-IN

Diapered in hospital linen,
my public seam stitched back into secrets,
I itch and heal in my crib, wrapped
in scopolamine. My lips like asbestos,
I can't make it
out of the medicine. Something has happened:
my belly has gone
flaccid, ersatz as sponge. Screwed
on this centripetal ache, I fix on pain
and breathe it like an element.
My neighbor-women are bad-mouthing the mothers-
in-law whose sons brought them to this.
We've been had. Joyful and dopey
we roll in our girlish paranoias.
The nurses want to sleep with the doctor; they wait
for my blood pressure to go down.
I try to climb, the walls shrug me off.
In my unique visiting hour I am visited
with guests witty beyond belief; before I can answer
the drug subsides, those pretend bastards are gone.

Back in my skull, out of love with the obstetrician,
I read my tag to prove I'm sensible.
The orderly wheels me upstairs to meet my daughter.

Funnyface, sweet heart,
this ordeal has almost nothing to do with love.

CITY PIGEONS

Old people are like birds:
the same words flock to the mind's eye
in speaking of them.
They perch in public places,
scratch for the world's crumbs, seek
its shiny trifles—
easily ruffled
are quick to realight, alert
and nodding,
cheeky occupants of plazas,
monuments' companions, suppliants
in lime-specked groves
to dirty mysteries.

A BEAUTIFUL VIEW
FROM THE WRONG PLACE

(Menemsha, Martha's Vineyard)

We are not where we thought; the path
misled us. We meant to be elsewhere; instead
we emerged above the harbor.
It is lovely here, though not
what we expected. Gray shacks squat
by the sea. We squint
across dunes into the sea's glitter,
eye-biting water of no color: not blue,
not green, but brighter. I taste
saltcracked lips. Thirst is the ocean's gift,
like this suddenly beautiful view
from the wrong place,
like love's gift.

DOCTOR, I GO

Doctor, I go vertical into my days:
managing, managing,
propped in my sensible arrangements,
margarine grin of the cop-out blearing
my behavior. I never made trouble
or asked for candy. Now I want

all my small demands met at once. I want
some bright, irreducible
bonheur; and screw ease,
the educated guess, reasons
for not expecting too much,
and settling for less than the best
of less.

IN THE DEPTHS

Seaweed clots, anemones, medusas,
water jewels—vials
of venomous extracts, poison salts—
spill their stains like cordials.
Small fish feed and breathe, quiver,
breed, are schooled in this liquid
and die. Dark traces
of mysterious stuff sleep in the tide:
dead, practicing.

In another city you are real:
here you are not here. I have that
palpable as blood,
the sea's proportions body-locked,
damned out of taste.
Once all my senses' sense of you
spread into thirst.

SUMMING UP

Someone has my number, that blue indelible series,
each digit an informational bit, betraying
name, dependence, frequency and duration of
hopes. To the wise and inside eye
the final numeral admits
chronicity: at one with the manqué,
alltime small losers.
For example
gray rooming-house ladies confused by bundles of infancy
into a quick grab and speedy abandoning,
disabused of nursery dreams,
done in by their failed encounter with childcare;
or Senior Citizens with babysitter transistors,
waiting at park benches to be reclaimed.
All tired. Let down. And still compelled
into a last accounting, as if, collected in wards
and keeping-places, faced with themselves
or any semblance of authority
something could be recollected or said.
Clasping and unclasping, rambling, picking at covers,
they offer, over and over, *God knows I tried.*

THE GOD FROM THE WASHING MACHINE

I.   Pounding linen
       I crouch at the confluence of streams;
       bubbles rush and break into
       the current's lather.
       I carry my basket over the stones.
       Some days you come down to the shore
       where laundry spreads in the sun.

       The sky in this story is Aegean blue,
       the stones are slate blue,
       our sails dazzle.

II.   These cycles have names like hints of miracles
       or clues to rites of passage.
       I am supposed to be enamored
       of my enamel Charybdis. I think
       someone has figured out I think
       it's a uterus, and am hormonally compelled
       to focus on it like pseudocyesis,
       as if there could never be enough washdays
       for this humble, eternally detergent mom
       or that I whirl in my automatic
       need to launder time out of mind.

III. On weekday afternoons the tube chronicles
       doomed houses, inordinate desire, and serial
       comedowns. While children nap
       events unfold like a carpet, Greek key
       after Greek key. Taken out of our lives
       we are caught in the ritual
       happenings, the choric nets of honor and excess,
       to cry woe and give ourselves over
       to guilt work, dreams of how we live.

ALABAMA, 1964

At home, lounging on page one,
fatback necks screwed
in an occasional slow swivel,
they stare from wirephotos as if they knew me
and spit suggestions like jets of tobacco.
They are casual, but ready for action.
(I would fold and sag
into dying—disappointed, rabbitty.)
Last night they moved into
a Boston minister:
his chipped skull and smashed breathing
bear witness to trouble in Selma.
He lies wrapped up in Birmingham
in very critical condition.
I am afraid, but bandaged in bulletins.
The early news mentions the *cruelty*
of breakthrough, as if
militant in our hope but knowing how things are
we should expect to pay in bodies.

POST PARTUM

(For Gillian Wolfe, born January 1967)

Small recapitulation, you swam in your salt
tidewater pool, summing up, doing your imitation
of history, exchanging substances in a selfish bubble
while your onlookers ballooned, expecting

(in your marine condition
you'd have been fitted gill-and-tail for escape)

as if you had given promises or agreed
to more than deliverance
or as if your new inabilities were a yes.

Whereas, after your fact, we
(surprised into capitulation)
unburden, seeing you come into your own
person, kindred and strange. Given
your singular version of the familiar
we admit it for what it is.
Tadpole, dear daughter,
Gillian, we want
what you are, and what follows
from that.

LEAVING, OR BEING LEFT

In the end, daisy clouds
peel across the sky:
a friend has moved on to what
friends move on to; and I
do heart's arithmetic on the proud,
laundered, but common petals:

he loves, he loves me not.

RIPLEY'S BELIEVE IT OR NOT

Health-ridden, uneasily normal, I sneak into this catalogue
of curiosities, accidents, mistakes,
pathological attempts and maimed solutions
and historical shockers—
Lincoln was wrong! He claimed
the world will little note nor long remember what we say here—
alongside tidbits stable and reversible as truth
(Name no one man. Able was I ere I saw Elba.),
records for brevity and size,
failed ambitions, sex gone bad, uncivilized responses
and collective extremities, alongside
glories of man and God: chasm,
edifice, compelling task, amazing ritual,
and strange praise.

            Like God, my doubts
are irrelevant to this compendium,
can't withstand the consistently astounding voice
riddled with exclamations, the tone
of coincidence worried into revelation
and white man's burden. I gasp
at each aborigine, hindoo, hideous
physiognomy, living death.
Here are my dark anxieties made graphic
as Angkor Wat: life is so various,
so possible, so close to impossible.

4 JANUARY 1965

Wind has cut four days of thin sun
out of the year, and scattered snow,
etching lace in the dry gutters,
acid openwork, as if
the ocean had come in this far,
placed its polite doilies
and receded

or some careless terminal case,
leaking from his ultimate wound
into the cold, had passed.

COMING CLOSE

After a while it was always the same
catch in imagination, the failure
to name sins, the relieved catalogue
of minor complaints: his relatives, her
foggy thinking; and the aggrieved tone.
But once, dramatic and appealing, daddy
pitched a cup of tea, which missed.
It splotched the shade:
the remnant of a kamikaze bat, or one
whose sonar went suddenly rabid and smashed him
into a Rorschach.
Or one who turned rodent-crazy
in mid-air.

Sometimes I'm happy: la la la la la la la
la la la la la la la la la la la la la la la la
la la la la. Tum tum ti tum. La la la la la la
la la la la la la la la la la la la la la la la.
Hey nonny nonny. La la la la la la la la la
la la la la la la la la la la la. Vo do di o do.
Poo poo pi doo. La la la la la la la la la la
la la la la la la la la la la la la la la la la
la la. Whack a doo. La la la la la la la. Sh-
boom, sh-boom. La la la la la la la la la la
la la la la la la la la la la la la la la la la
la la. Dum di dum. La la la la la la la la la
la la la la la la la la la. Tra la la. Tra la la
la la la la la la la la la la. Yeah yeah yeah.

LOVE'S GAME: *GO*

The stones
of separate colors
defeat me.
I have no such thoughts.

Telling the stones
like rosaries:
you, you, you.

I am bound to lose
this game.
I do not choose
to avoid
enclosure.

You may increase the space
tenfold;
never enough.

The first move: complete
statement. Others
merely repeat.

AN APPRECIATION

Daddy, I paid for your errors; now
you are supporting mine, keeping me
safe against mistaken investments, innocent
in my history of wrong choice.
After all, I ought to tell
how I go deeper into
love on our mutual, infinite accounts.

After all the trivial gifts and misgivings
I whirl in our blood circle like the king's daughter
in her bride-price, treasured and understood.

NIJINSKY

I. Taking the Pros to Dine

When, amid red velvet decor and deluxe leavings
of your gift, the whores pushed back their platters
and stripped, their after-dinner thanks
turned your stomach. Did you expect
a graceful speech, sweetly passing the mints,
or that, a mass elevation, they would rise
en point, a healthy corps de ballet, and execute
L'Après-Midi d'un Faun, redeemed by Art?
You had no heart for professionals, and fled
the painted faces and swollen, beckoning arms
in a deep sickening of pity and rage, a thwarted
love, misunderstood. Receiving right payment
and thinking yourself God, you never considered
the limits of performance.

II. Taking Steps

Despite your insane attacks
and warding off, the unbalanced positions,
you knew evil and tried
to answer. Seeing the agonies and plagues
you went vegetarian and wrote *love, love,
love:* it seeped out of your journal,
a hemorrhage, while you danced like the wounded negro
in *Schéhérazade.* Laying about with your love you struck
and struck, admitting no exceptions, grieving for wife,
czar, whores, the poor, even the impresario
who loved boys and must be stopped—
the bad, trapped, and disinherited.
Trained in the imperial economics of pain

you determined to make a killing
in Zurich, and then destroy the Stock Exchange
although you were without
German—but never went, or saved a soul
or convinced anyone that you mourned for their reasons.
My madness is my love towards mankind.
That mad love of men
is a kind of doom, and you traveled into your passion.
I am a wounded bull, I am God in the bull, an Egyptian,
a Red Indian, a Negro, a Chinaman, a Japanese, a foreigner,
a stranger, a sea bird, a land bird.
Until, driving your body, that perfect
and wretched instrument, through waist-high snow
you fell like a stricken horse, incapable.
Trying to save you, they locked you
in the house of dead miseries.

III. World War I and Later

I have drawn a picture of Christ without moustaches and
beard, with long hair. I look like Him; only He has a calm
gaze and my eyes look round. I am a man of motion, *not one*
of immobility. I have different habits from Christ. He loved
immobility, and I love motion and dancing.

The Diary of Vaslav Nijinsky

Practiced in bad habits, he moved from the apprehension
of love to assault, took God
for his Hostage, using Him for purposes—
making that human condition of mutual faggotry
a divine union, a sacred activity

man-to-man, the ultimate
in relations. During the long morning, after
the dancing was over and conflicts opened
in their awful choreography, he could not fail
to make connections; mouthing the Word
as if it were his own, and then a self,
his final, incredible leap freed him
to acknowledge the diary: God and Nijinsky, 1919.

IV. Saying It

*My little girl is singing: 'Ah, ah, ah, ah, ah!' I
do not understand its meaning, but I feel what
she wants to say. She wants to say that every-
thing—Ah! Ah!—is not horror but joy.*
                    The Diary of Vaslav Nijinsky

His syllabic chaos:
all words the same
expulsion of breath—ah!—the fatal music.
Released from parts of speech
he was alive, each wound
an evidence. Pain circled like God's blood:
trying to name the unspeakable pulse: joy.

SPECULATION ON THE
BOSTON STRANGLER

Behind my door, I am interested
to know he saunters
through the metropolis, comicbook figure
in a flashy comeback, catering
to my vulgar hopes: out there
for everyone, he loiters in a common agony,
acting out dreams of the fatal passion,
the helpless attack.
I am interested to know
if this one is only human, and if
this once he could be saved if someone
loved him enough, enough, enough.

AFTER TERMINATION

Doctor, you probably suspect
with reason
our midnight conversations, shorthand jokes
and coded mumbles, me plugged into
your secret broadcasts, screwed by the ears
and answering back—gutsy girl!—spilling
the magic beans, fingering connections.
My stereo jiminy cricket furry mother, my
middleman, wiseguy, head:
oh, stubborn—you persist
year to year in love's position:
being there.

TAKING THE TRIP

Dreaming of God-knows-what they turn on
and see God, half in and half
out of their minds. They claim they can
smell evil and understand words. What
illegal luck. I stay within
the statutes. But

at night, without benefit
of communion or send-off
I am God the menace, network,
victim, mommy, and pay-off,
split into visited and visiting,
having traveled the route to Wits End.

ON STARTING AT NURSERY SCHOOL

(To D.J.C.)

"Play is a child's work."
Darling, they
will cram your sweet head
with importances, in the way
of teachers, educate the senses
by blocks and fingerpaint pretenses,
refine, instruct under the guise
of games. Darling, I submit
that, taken by surprise,
you will take to it.

SEEING YOU OFF

Goodbyes precipitate in the stale air like a threat
of rain: perpetual terminal weather.
Making headway, rushing against
our will, we pass the long cars, dodging puddles
and baggage carts, sidestepping flocks of pigeons and
nuns—dark ladies
of the railways—to lounge in the leftover atmosphere
of leavetaking. The train stands like a fixture;
in its shadow we make a conversation.

Amid comings and goings, caught in this re-enactment,
we try to avoid a scene. Too late. Being here
we are in it: a station, a departure, another loss
continuing a history of losses. *Again,*
again. Never repaid with any return. Obedient
we wait for the signal.
In our nervous to-and-fro we circle for time,
mentioning other travels, tracking periodic pain
like a reassurance. *Aboard!* At least
the last-minute scramble, mumbled *take care,*
platform jumbling with sudden moves, a kind of arrival.
The train gains ground. I fall back
into the good behavior of those left behind.

CROSSES

I wish you in the sea, said the Knight upon the road,
  With a good boat under me, said the child as he stood.
I think I hear a bell, said the Knight upon the road,
  And it's tolling thee to Hell, said the child as he stood.

Voices fill the dark air with a deep language,
spelling the unspeakable into a jumble.
The unnameable rises from covens and rides,
inviting intercourse, circling for damage.
Fixing in a continual X, ever and ever
ready to ward off evil
the voices pronounce their innocence.
Answering witchy exercise, checking
the devil's sortilège: we are silver
and safe with our amulets, crossing the Night.

THE HIPPIES OF HARVARD SQUARE

My goggle-eyed angels, you stare
at a tinted world, swing and rock
on the balls of your feet, sweethearts,
twitching your bony shoulders like secret wings,
beatling in denim suits and granny smocks.
The urge to frug into your vinyl colors
pumps like music. Even the menace of black leather
is touching. It would be tactless
to fling myself into your willowing hair or fall
at your boots, but you are a hard act to follow
hands-off. I settle for loving
the sight of you.

                Peering through wire rims
you seem heaven-sent to record mundane happenings.
But *you* are the visual event, the self-made
signs of grace, advertisement
for the Absurd made flesh, your own
revelation, the funny miracle.

AN EMPTY BED AT THE ASYLUM

I ought to be there:
hair snakes coiled about my poor skull,
headaches from bad thoughts
and bad air
and shrieks flung past mad brains.

In my mother's print
the inmates of Saint Luke's writhe
and clutch and wrench themselves to pieces.
Unmoved by time and unrestrained by art
they posture in their gorgeous agonies
throughout my childhood.

The girl I was paces dank halls
past skeleton faces
and devil'd bodies hurled like weapons
against stone walls.

I should be there now;
some lunatic hope commits me to escape.
I will not get far: unconfined,
I cannot get out of myself
and will return to arrange myself
among the frenzied statuary of my own mind.

IN COMMUNICATION WITH A UFO

Objects clutter the shiny air and flash
through the night sky, parsing its darkness
into the telegraphic grammar of space:

Here! We are here! Believe!
We hover but will not fix, we wheel
in the skeptical atmosphere. Beyond the reach
of your vision we skim curves of the universe
and splash like otters in its large drafts,
uttering shrieks of light, bellywhopping
to where you hang. Each sighting irks you
into a flurry of hope. Blind
with anticipation, earthlings, you want us
to be serious, bring the good news, disclose
that we are what you want us to be.

LOOKING OUT

Mother, I am something more
than your girl; still our old quarrel
brings me up.
A Miss Universe parade of ex-wives,
marketers, secretaries, park ladies
with prams, mistresses,
fiancées, mysterious female lives
shimmer and ache against my sight
like migraine.

        The world
is half full of women, each
a face of our argument,
each with ex-husband,
dinner guest, boss, lover,
or no one. Sisters,
enemies: some might understand that
attached, varied, and secret,
they are my battle.

MYTHICS

(To R.S.F.)

I. Ondine

All the cautionary tales of strange girls
could not prevent coming to this:
sea-changed, I dance in shallows
dripping feathery anklets
and splash in the tide (foamy,
opalescent) weedy hair eddying
in its elemental pull,
the fish princess who asked for legs
and bled into her footprints,
her scaly heart flaking until dawn.

II. Cinderella

In this domicile of cosmetic disasters
(dowager's hump, psoriasis, spinster's
breath, dropped arches) I queen it
over the slag heap, over the resident
hags. None of theirs! Changeling
beauty, domestic burden: I sift coal
like black diamonds—alien, determined
to make it out of this dreary household.

III. Rapunzel

Removed by that crone
I range in my cloister, closeted with
dreams of release, growing my hair
like foliage, gathering moss.
Ugly, covetous, my keeper rages at her ward,
her golden girl. Our bramble thickets lock

into a wall and darken my chamber.
You might find me
and I unbraid to your call,
glory in the fall of my crowning glory,
drop into living with my blind, punished hero.

IV. Rumpelstiltskin

I took instruction in love's ravel,
fabricated a homespun treasure
and dazzled my greedy regent into husbandry.
After the baby, complications set in.
Pursued by my useful, anonymous menace
and spinning frantic names, I twisted
in our blood bargain until a minister
told his funny story: how
the little man wove his grotesque forest circle,
the gleeful warp of my answer.
And when, dancing into a tantrum
he dropped out of the riddle
I kept my king, gold, child, and secret.

V. Snow White

Fled from the battle, hid
from the wicked queen's fatal plot,
I lie low and make do
with beauty and virtue
and cohabit with small men: friendly,
inadequate. This house,
my woodsy retreat, is easy
to keep in order. What could be more

innocent, except to dream,
latent and clothed, under glass
until the prince and his retinue
jar my crib and I am aroused,
passive, saved?

VI. Psyche

In these nights, transported, I know
love's perfection: words like the heart's choke,
body's language, framed like a dream,
the ultimate dark secret.
Women have risked burning
for hours less extraordinary than these.
Love, waiting for your visit
I long for the dailiness, human rubs, usual
trials and flawed pleasures
this perpetual ecstasy denies.

VII. Beauty (and the Beast)

Whether it was the maxims about good hearts
and the limited value of pure esthetics
or something closer to danger—
once I saw him, the princelings and precepts went
neutral as oatmeal. He was ugly as sin:
animal heavings, flaccid mouth, agonized baboon stare,
pitted skin, hairshirted like a mistaken birth.
My cry mimicked pity.
Ladies, all's fair in
ignorance; I was young and easily moved.
Now, rewarded, I submit to his transfiguration.

STRENGTH

Lord, surely you took the position designed to infuriate
and held it until the end
when you spread your arms in a blessing
and gesture of union with the assemblage of comrades, catching
and hauling them like fish in the enraging net
of your unconditional love.
From the beginning, above all suffering all,
unweaponed, you opened and shrugged
into your inhuman posture

which was unlikeable:
a cellular message, the adrenalin clue
for animals met on disputed ground,
the stance that triggers attack. Words
are too recent a skill to do good—we decode
bodies.

      A Buddhist monk on the cover of *Life* droops
on his shadow like a man on a cross;
quiet men walk into flak. In a primitive language
they ask for it. The undefended stand
like victims. Signalling *unfit!* mistaken
for fair game, the loving unfold.
Christ I could have told you how few
would be pacified.

NAPALM

The children bud into flame.
They flare and char, time-lapsed
in a bright eye.

        Among growing things
the hellblooms' cycle of quickening and blaze
is unique. Saved from decay, the withered fall,
they are the glories of morning and total celebrants
of high noon.

        Like small petals of sun
they open and burn, as if all their purposes
were in that burning.

GETTING THE NEWS

There's no sense in listening to it, except
that it's really happening.

In the crazy house it's easy
to trust the bulletins: everyone's doing well, considering
what everyone's doing here.

Dear Mom, a lady asked me how I was.
When I (after I flicked the bugs
off my arm) told her she said I shouldn't think
in terms of that word, dear,
it wasn't useful. But. Who's
taking care of whom? Please send
something.

Places are situations.
Everyone turns in his own bed, out
of sight, out of mind. Some acts
are more insane than others.
Where are the soldiers, and those gone mad
from giving the facts?

Man, what goes on here is where it's at.
Like when this cat jammed the broadcast
from the lightbulbs and tried to shove something
up my veins, the whole time
pushing love like it was H—crazy!

In the asylum they put easy questions
(the year, the President), but no one says
Fit them together, Make them mean,
Move the scalded babies to where you live.

ENCOUNTERS AND

A sacred being cannot be anticipated—it must be encountered.

W. H. Auden

Suddenly met, unaccountably set into my hours
you are entirely here
paired with your palpable absence,
particled as air.
Without knowing you I could not imagine you
gone.

You are a gift, a grief, a gift,
a possible final grief

like the Chinese nests
whose diminishing answers suggest infinite loss.